ARTIFICIAL INTELLIGENCE FOUNDATIONS

About the Tutorial

This tutorial provides introductory knowledge on Artificial Intelligence. It would come to a great help if you are about to select Artificial Intelligence as a course subject. You can briefly know about the areas of AI in which research is prospering.

Audience

This tutorial is prepared for the students at beginner level who aspire to learn Artificial Intelligence.

Prerequisites

The basic knowledge of Computer Science is mandatory. The knowledge of Mathematics, Languages, Science, Mechanical or Electrical engineering is a plus.

Table of Contents

1. Overview of AI

Since the invention of computers or machines, their capability to perform various tasks went on growing exponentially. Humans have developed the power of computer systems in terms of their diverse working domains, their increasing speed, and reducing size with respect to time.

A branch of Computer Science named *Artificial Intelligence* pursues creating the computers or machines as intelligent as human beings.

What is Artificial Intelligence?

According to the father of Artificial Intelligence John McCarthy, it is *"The science and engineering of making intelligent machines, especially intelligent computer programs"*.

Artificial Intelligence is a way of **making a computer, a computer-controlled robot, or a software think intelligently**, in the similar manner the intelligent humans think.

AI is accomplished by studying how human brain thinks, and how humans learn, decide, and work while trying to solve a problem, and then using the outcomes of this study as a basis of developing intelligent software and systems.

Philosophy of AI

While exploiting the power of the computer systems, the curiosity of human, lead him to wonder, "Can a machine think and behave like humans do?"

Thus, the development of AI started with the intention of creating similar intelligence in machines that we find and regard high in humans.

Goals of AI

- **To Create Expert Systems:** The systems which exhibit intelligent behavior, learn, demonstrate, explain, and advice its users.

- **To Implement Human Intelligence in Machines:** Creating systems that understand, think, learn, and behave like humans.

What Contributes to AI?

Artificial intelligence is a science and technology based on disciplines such as Computer Science, Biology, Psychology, Linguistics, Mathematics, and Engineering. A major thrust of AI is in the development of computer functions associated with human intelligence, such as reasoning, learning, and problem solving.

Out of the following areas, one or multiple areas can contribute to build an intelligent system.

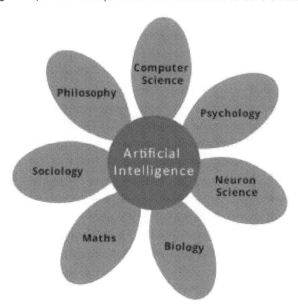

Programming Without and With AI

The programming without and with AI is different in following ways:

Programming Without AI	Programming With AI
A computer program without AI can answer the **specific** questions it is meant to solve.	A computer program with AI can answer the **generic** questions it is meant to solve.
Modification in the program leads to change in its structure.	AI programs can absorb new modifications by putting highly independent pieces of information together. Hence you can modify even a minute piece of information of program without affecting its structure.
Modification is not quick and easy. It may lead to affecting the program adversely.	Quick and Easy program modification.

2

What is AI Technique?

In the real world, the knowledge has some unwelcomed properties:

- Its volume is huge, next to unimaginable.
- It is not well-organized or well-formatted.
- It keeps changing constantly.

AI Technique is a manner to organize and use the knowledge efficiently in such a way that:

- It should be perceivable by the people who provide it.
- It should be easily modifiable to correct errors.
- It should be useful in many situations though it is incomplete or inaccurate.

AI techniques elevate the speed of execution of the complex program it is equipped with.

Applications of AI

AI has been dominant in various fields such as:

- **Gaming**

  AI plays crucial role in strategic games such as chess, poker, tic-tac-toe, etc., where machine can think of large number of possible positions based on heuristic knowledge.

- **Natural Language Processing**

  It is possible to interact with the computer that understands natural language spoken by humans.

- **Expert Systems**

  There are some applications which integrate machine, software, and special information to impart reasoning and advising. They provide explanation and advice to the users.

- **Vision Systems**

  These systems understand, interpret, and comprehend visual input on the computer. For example,

  - A spying aeroplane takes photographs which are used to figure out spatial information or map of the areas.
  - Doctors use clinical expert system to diagnose the patient.
  - Police use computer software that can recognize the face of criminal with the stored portrait made by forensic artist.

- **Speech Recognition**

  Some intelligent systems are capable of hearing and comprehending the language in terms of sentences and their meanings while a human talks to it. It can handle different accents, slang words, noise in the background, change in human's noise due to cold, etc.

- **Handwriting Recognition**

  The handwriting recognition software reads the text written on paper by a pen or on screen by a stylus. It can recognize the shapes of the letters and convert it into editable text.

- **Intelligent Robots**

  Robots are able to perform the tasks given by a human. They have sensors to detect physical data from the real world such as light, heat, temperature, movement, sound, bump, and pressure. They have efficient processors, multiple sensors and huge memory, to exhibit intelligence. In addition, they are capable of learning from their mistakes and they can adapt to the new environment.

History of AI

Here is the history of AI during 20th century:

Year	Milestone / Innovation
1923	Karel Čapek's play named "Rossum's Universal Robots" (RUR) opens in London, first use of the word "robot" in English.
1943	Foundations for neural networks laid.
1945	Isaac Asimov, a Columbia University alumni, coined the term *Robotics*.
1950	Alan Turing introduced Turing Test for evaluation of intelligence and published *Computing Machinery and Intelligence.* Claude Shannon published *Detailed Analysis of Chess Playing* as a search.
1956	John McCarthy coined the term *Artificial Intelligence.* Demonstration of the first running AI program at Carnegie Mellon University.
1958	John McCarthy invents LISP programming language for AI.
1964	Danny Bobrow's dissertation at MIT showed that computers can understand natural language well enough to solve algebra word problems correctly.
1965	Joseph Weizenbaum at MIT built *ELIZA*, an interactive problem that carries on a dialogue in English.
1969	Scientists at Stanford Research Institute Developed *Shakey*, a robot, equipped with locomotion, perception, and problem solving.

1973	The Assembly Robotics group at Edinburgh University built *Freddy*, the Famous Scottish Robot, capable of using vision to locate and assemble models.
1979	The first computer-controlled autonomous vehicle, Stanford Cart, was built.
1985	Harold Cohen created and demonstrated the drawing program, *Aaron*.
1990	Major advances in all areas of AI: • Significant demonstrations in machine learning • Case-based reasoning • Multi-agent planning • Scheduling • Data mining, Web Crawler • natural language understanding and translation • Vision, Virtual Reality • Games
1997	The Deep Blue Chess Program beats the then world chess champion, Garry Kasparov.
2000	Interactive robot pets become commercially available. MIT displays *Kismet*, a robot with a face that expresses emotions. The robot *Nomad* explores remote regions of Antarctica and locates meteorites.

2. Intelligent Systems

While studying artificially intelligence, you need to know what intelligence is. This chapter covers Idea of intelligence, types, and components of intelligence.

What is Intelligence?

The ability of a system to calculate, reason, perceive relationships and analogies, learn from experience, store and retrieve information from memory, solve problems, comprehend complex ideas, use natural language fluently, classify, generalize, and adapt new situations.

Types of Intelligence

As described by Howard Gardner, an American developmental psychologist, the Intelligence comes in multifold:

Intelligence	Description	Example
Linguistic intelligence	The ability to speak, recognize, and use mechanisms of phonology (speech sounds), syntax (grammar), and semantics (meaning).	Narrators, Orators
Musical intelligence	The ability to create, communicate with, and understand meanings made of sound, understanding of pitch, rhythm.	Musicians, Singers, Composers
Logical-mathematical intelligence	The ability of use and understand relationships in the absence of action or objects. Understanding complex and abstract ideas.	Mathematicians, Scientists
Spatial intelligence	The ability to perceive visual or spatial information, change it, and re-create visual images without reference to the objects, construct 3D images, and to move and rotate them.	Map readers, Astronauts, Physicists
Bodily-Kinesthetic intelligence	The ability to use complete or part of the body to solve problems or fashion products, control over fine and coarse motor skills, and manipulate the objects.	Players, Dancers
Intra-personal intelligence	The ability to distinguish among one's own feelings, intentions, and motivations.	Gautam Buddha

Interpersonal intelligence	The ability to recognize and make distinctions among other people's feelings, beliefs, and intentions.	Mass Communicators, Interviewers

You can say a machine or a system is **artificially intelligent** when it is equipped with at least one and at most all intelligences in it.

What is Intelligence Composed of?

The intelligence is intangible. It is composed of:

1. Reasoning
2. Learning
3. Problem Solving
4. Perception
5. Linguistic Intelligence

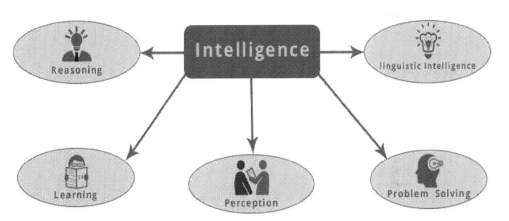

Let us go through all the components briefly:

1. **Reasoning:** It is the set of processes that enables us to provide basis for judgement, making decisions, and prediction. There are broadly two types:

Inductive Reasoning	Deductive Reasoning
It conducts specific observations to makes broad general statements.	It starts with a general statement and examines the possibilities to reach a specific, logical conclusion.
Even if all of the premises are true in a statement, inductive reasoning allows for the conclusion to be false.	If something is true of a class of things in general, it is also true for all members of that class.

Example:	Example:
"Nita is a teacher.	"All women of age above 60 years are
All teachers are studious.	grandmothers.
Therefore, Nita is studious."	Shalini is 65 years.
	Therefore, Shalini is a grandmother."

2. **Learning:** It is the activity of gaining knowledge or skill by studying, practising, being taught, or experiencing something. Learning enhances the awareness of the subjects of the study.

   The ability of learning is possessed by humans, some animals, and AI-enabled systems. Learning is categorized as:

   o **Auditory Learning:** It is learning by listening and hearing. For example, students listening to recorded audio lectures.

   o **Episodic Learning:** To learn by remembering sequences of events that one has witnessed or experienced. This is linear and orderly.

   o **Motor Learning:** It is learning by precise movement of muscles. For example, picking objects, Writing, etc.

   o **Observational Learning:** To learn by watching and imitating others. For example, child tries to learn by mimicking her parent.

   o **Perceptual Learning:** It is learning to recognize stimuli that one has seen before. For example, identifying and classifying objects and situations.

   o **Relational Learning:** It involves learning to differentiate among various stimuli on the basis of relational properties, rather than absolute properties. For Example, Adding 'little less' salt at the time of cooking potatoes that came up salty last time, when cooked with adding say a tablespoon of salt.

   o **Spatial learning:** It is learning through visual stimuli such as images, colors, maps, etc. For Example, A person can create roadmap in mind before actually following the road.

   o **Stimulus-Response Learning:** It is learning to perform a particular behavior when a certain stimulus is present. For example, a dog raises its ear on hearing doorbell.

3. **Problem solving:** It is the process in which one perceives and tries to arrive at a desired solution from a present situation by taking some path, which is blocked by known or unknown hurdles.

   Problem solving also includes **decision making,** which is the process of selecting the best suitable alternative out of multiple alternatives to reach the desired goal are available.

4. **Perception**: It is the process of acquiring, interpreting, selecting, and organizing sensory information.

Perception presumes **sensing**. In humans, perception is aided by sensory organs. In the domain of AI, perception mechanism puts the data acquired by the sensors together in a meaningful manner.

5. **Linguistic Intelligence:** It is one's ability to use, comprehend, speak, and write the verbal and written language. It is important in interpersonal communication.

Difference between Human and Machine Intelligence

- Humans perceive by patterns whereas the machines perceive by set of rules and data.

- Humans store and recall information by patterns, machines do it by searching algorithms. For example, the number 40404040 is easy to remember, store and recall as its pattern is simple.

- Humans can figure out the complete object even if some part of it is missing or distorted; whereas the machines cannot correctly.

3.   Research Areas of AI

The domain of artificial intelligence is huge in breadth and width. While proceeding, we consider the broadly common and prospering research areas in the domain of AI:

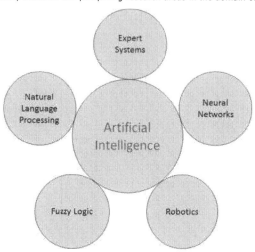

Speech and Voice Recognition

These both terms are common in robotics, expert systems and natural language processing. Though these terms are used interchangeably, their objectives are different.

Speech Recognition	Voice Recognition
The speech recognition aims at understanding and comprehending WHAT was spoken.	The objective of voice recognition is to recognize WHO is speaking.
It is used in hand-free computing, map or menu navigation	It analyzes person's tone, voice pitch, and accent, etc., to identify a person.
Machine does not need training as it is not speaker dependent.	The recognition system needs training as it is person-oriented.

Speaker independent Speech Recognition systems are difficult to develop.	Speaker-dependent Speech Recognition systems are comparatively easy to develop.

Working of Speech and Voice Recognition Systems

The user input spoken at a microphone goes to sound card of the system. The converter turns the analog signal into equivalent digital signal for the speech processing. The database is used to compare the patterns to recognize the words. Finally, a reverse feedback is given to the database.

This source-language text becomes input to the Translation Engine, which converts it to the target language text. They are supported with interactive GUI, large database of vocabulary etc.

Real Life Applications of Research Areas

There is a large array of applications where AI is serving common people in their day-to-day lives:

Sr. No.	Research Area	Real Life Application
1	**Expert Systems** **Examples**: Flight-tracking systems, Clinical systems	
2	**Natural Language Processing** **Examples**: Google Now feature, speech recognition, Automatic voice output	
3	**Neural Networks** **Examples**: Pattern recognition systems such as face recognition, character recognition, handwriting recognition.	

4	**Robotics** **Examples**: Industrial robots for moving, spraying, painting, precision checking, drilling, cleaning, coating, carving etc.	
5	**Fuzzy Logic** **Examples**: Consumer electronics, automobiles, etc.	

Task Classification of AI

The domain of AI is classified into *Formal* tasks, *Mundane* tasks, and *Expert* tasks.

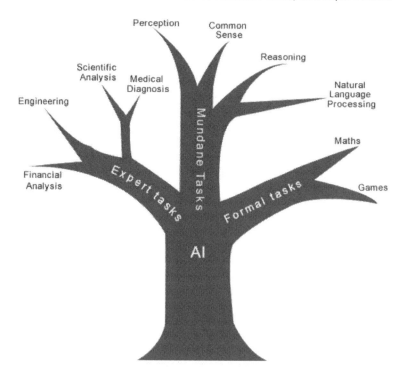

Task Domains of Artificial Intelligence		
Mundane (Ordinary) Tasks	Formal Tasks	Expert Tasks
Perception • Computer Vision • Speech, Voice	• Mathematics • Geometry • Logic • Integration and Differentiation	• Engineering • Fault finding • Manufacturing • Monitoring
Natural Language Processing • Understanding • Language Generation • Language Translation	Games • Go • Chess (Deep Blue) • Checkers	Scientific Analysis
Common Sense	Verification	Financial Analysis
Reasoning	Theorem Proving	Medical Diagnosis
Planning		Creativity
Robotics • Locomotive		

Humans learn **mundane (ordinary) tasks** since their birth. They learn by perception, speaking, using language, and locomotives. They learn Formal Tasks and Expert Tasks later, in that order.

For humans, the mundane tasks are easiest to learn. The same was considered true before trying to implement mundane tasks in machines. Earlier, all work of AI was concentrated in the mundane task domain.

Later, it turned out that the machine requires more knowledge, complex knowledge representation, and complicated algorithms for handling mundane tasks. This is the reason **why AI work is more prospering in the Expert Task** domain now, as the expert task domain needs expert knowledge without common sense, which can be easier to represent and handle.

4. Agents and Environments

An AI system is composed of an agent and its environment. The agents act in their environment. The environment may contain other agents.

What are Agent and Environment?

An **agent** is anything that can perceive its environment through **sensors** and acts upon that **environment** through **effectors**.

- A **human agent** has sensory organs such as eyes, ears, nose, tongue and skin parallel to the sensors, and other organs such as hands, legs, mouth, for effectors.
- A **robotic agent** replaces cameras and infrared range finders for the sensors, and various motors and actuators for effectors.
- A **software agent** has encoded bit strings as its programs and actions.

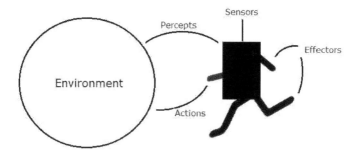

Agents Terminology

- **Performance Measure of Agent:** It is the criteria, which determines how successful an agent is.
- **Behavior of Agent:** It is the action that agent performs after any given sequence of percepts.
- **Percept**: It is agent's perceptual inputs at a given instance.
- **Percept Sequence:** It is the history of all that an agent has perceived till date.

- **Agent Function:** It is a map from the precept sequence to an action.

Rationality

Rationality is nothing but status of being reasonable, sensible, and having good sense of judgment.

Rationality is concerned with expected actions and results depending upon what the agent has perceived. Performing actions with the aim of obtaining useful information is an important part of rationality.

What is Ideal Rational Agent?

An ideal rational agent is the one, which is capable of doing expected actions to maximize its performance measure, on the basis of:

- Its percept sequence
- Its built-in knowledge base

Rationality of an agent depends on the following:

1. The **performance measures**, which determine the degree of success.
2. Agent's **Percept Sequence** till now.
3. The agent's **prior knowledge about the environment**.
4. The **actions** that the agent can carry out.

A rational agent always performs right action, where the right action means the action that causes the agent to be most successful in the given percept sequence. The problem the agent solves is characterized by Performance Measure, Environment, Actuators, and Sensors (PEAS).

The Structure of Intelligent Agents

Agent's structure can be viewed as:

- Agent = Architecture + Agent Program
- Architecture = the machinery that an agent executes on.
- Agent Program = an implementation of an agent function.

Simple Reflex Agents

- They choose actions only based on the current percept.
- They are rational only if a correct decision is made only on the basis of current precept.
- Their environment is completely observable.

Condition-Action Rule – It is a rule that maps a state (condition) to an action.

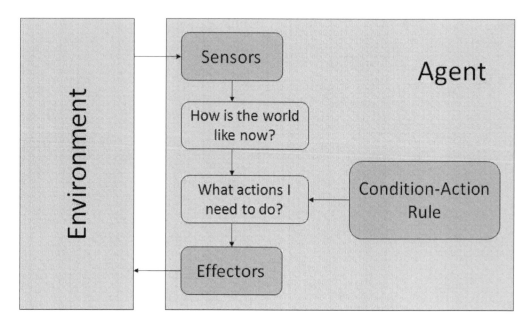

Model-Based Reflex Agents

They use a model of the world to choose their actions. They maintain an internal state.

Model: knowledge about "how the things happen in the world".

Internal State: It is a representation of unobserved aspects of current state depending on percept history.

Updating state requires the information about

- How the world evolves.
- How the agent's actions affect the world.

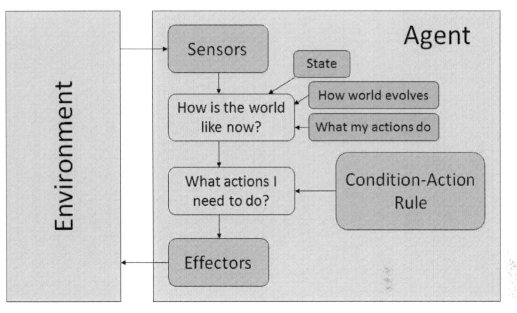

Goal-Based Agents

They choose their actions in order to achieve goals. Goal-based approach is more flexible than reflex agent since the knowledge supporting a decision is explicitly modeled, thereby allowing for modifications.

- **Goal:** It is the description of desirable situations.

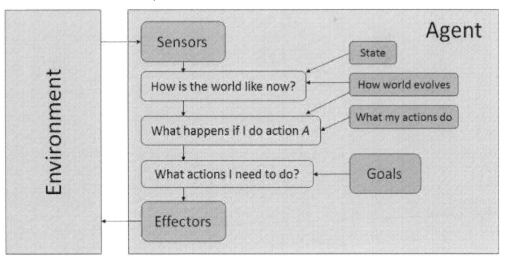

Utility-Based Agents

They choose actions based on a preference (utility) for each state.

Goals are inadequate when:

- There are conflicting goals only some of which can be achieved.
- Goals have some uncertainty of being achieved and one needs to weigh likelihood of success against the importance of a goal.

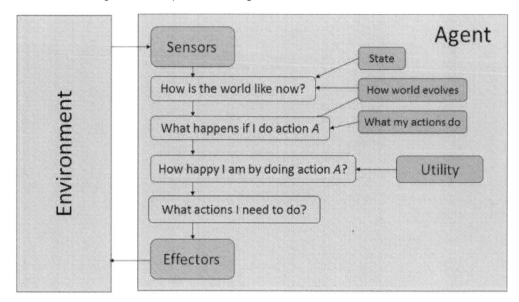

The Nature of Environments

Some programs operate in the entirely **artificial environment** confined to keyboard input, database, computer file systems and character output on a screen.

In contrast, some software agents (software robots or softbots) exist in rich, unlimited softbots domains. The simulator has a **very detailed, complex environment.** The software agent needs to choose from a long array of actions in real time. A softbot designed to scan the online preferences of the customer and show interesting items to the customer works in the **real** as well as an **artificial** environment.

The most famous **artificial environment** is the **Turing Test environment**, in which one real and other artificial agents are tested on equal ground. This is a very challenging environment as it is highly difficult for a software agent to perform as well as a human.

Turing Test

The success of an intelligent behavior of a system can be measured with Turing Test.

Two persons and a machine to be evaluated participate in the test. Out of the two persons, one plays the role of the tester. Each of them sits in different rooms. The tester is unaware of who is machine and who is a human. He interrogates the questions by typing and sending them to both intelligences, to which he receives typed responses.

This test aims at fooling the tester. If the tester fails to determine machine's response from the human response, then the machine is said to be intelligent.

Properties of Environment

The environment has multifold properties:

- **Discrete / Continuous:** If there are a limited number of distinct, clearly defined, states of the environment, the environment is discrete (For example, chess); otherwise it is continuous (For example, driving).

- **Observable / Partially Observable**: If it is possible to determine the complete state of the environment at each time point from the percepts it is observable; otherwise it is only partially observable.

- **Static / Dynamic**: If the environment does not change while an agent is acting, then it is static; otherwise it is dynamic.

- **Single agent / Multiple agents**: The environment may contain other agents which may be of the same or different kind as that of the agent.

- **Accessible vs. inaccessible**: If the agent's sensory apparatus can have access to the complete state of the environment, then the environment is accessible to that agent.

- **Deterministic vs. Non-deterministic**: If the next state of the environment is completely determined by the current state and the actions of the agent, then the environment is deterministic; otherwise it is non-deterministic.

- **Episodic vs. Non-episodic**: In an episodic environment, each episode consists of the agent perceiving and then acting. The quality of its action depends just on the episode itself. Subsequent episodes do not depend on the actions in the previous episodes. Episodic environments are much simpler because the agent does not need to think ahead.

5. Popular Search Algorithms

Searching is the universal technique of problem solving in AI. There are some single-player games such as tile games, Sudoku, crossword, etc. The search algorithms help you to search for a particular position in such games.

Single Agent Pathfinding Problems

The games such as 3X3 eight-tile, 4X4 fifteen-tile, and 5X5 twenty four tile puzzles are single-agent-path-finding challenges. They consist of a matrix of tiles with a blank tile. The player is required to arrange the tiles by sliding a tile either vertically or horizontally into a blank space with the aim of accomplishing some objective.

The other examples of single agent pathfinding problems are Travelling Salesman Problem, Rubik's Cube, and Theorem Proving.

Search Terminology

Problem Space: It is the environment in which the search takes place. (A set of states and set of operators to change those states)

Problem Instance: It is Initial state + Goal state

Problem Space Graph: It represents problem state. States are shown by nodes and operators are shown by edges.

Depth of a problem: Length of a shortest path or shortest sequence of operators from Initial State to goal state.

Space Complexity: The maximum number of nodes that are stored in memory.

Time Complexity: The maximum number of nodes that are created.

Admissibility: A property of an algorithm to always find an optimal solution.

Branching Factor: The average number of child nodes in the problem space graph.

Depth: Length of the shortest path from initial state to goal state.

Brute-Force Search Strategies

They are most simple, as they do not need any domain-specific knowledge. They work fine with small number of possible states.

Requirements –

- State description

- A set of valid operators
- Initial state
- Goal state description

Breadth-First Search

It starts from the root node, explores the neighboring nodes first and moves towards the next level neighbors. It generates one tree at a time until the solution is found. It can be implemented using FIFO queue data structure. This method provides shortest path to the solution.

If **branching factor** (average number of child nodes for a given node) = b and depth = d, then number of nodes at level d = b^d.

The total no of nodes created in worst case is $b + b^2 + b^3 + \ldots + b^d$.

Disadvantage: Since each level of nodes is saved for creating next one, it consumes a lot of memory space. Space requirement to store nodes is exponential.

Its complexity depends on the number of nodes. It can check duplicate nodes.

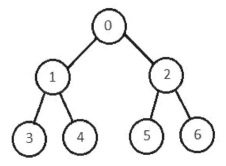

Depth-First Search

It is implemented in recursion with LIFO stack data structure. It creates the same set of nodes as Breadth-First method, only in the different order.

As the nodes on the single path are stored in each iteration from root to leaf node, the space requirement to store nodes is linear. With branching factor b and depth as m, the storage space is bm.

Disadvantage: This algorithm may not terminate and go on infinitely on one path. The solution to this issue is to choose a cut-off depth. If the ideal cut-off is d, and if chosen cut-off is lesser than d, then this algorithm may fail. If chosen cut-off is more than d, then execution time increases.

Its complexity depends on the number of paths. It cannot check duplicate nodes.

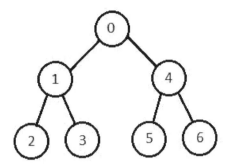

Bidirectional Search

It searches forward from initial state and backward from goal state till both meet to identify a common state.

The path from initial state is concatenated with the inverse path from the goal state. Each search is done only up to half of the total path.

Uniform Cost Search

Sorting is done in increasing cost of the path to a node. It always expands the least cost node. It is identical to Breadth First search if each transition has the same cost.

It explores paths in the increasing order of cost.

Disadvantage: There can be multiple long paths with the cost $\leq C^*$. Uniform Cost search must explore them all.

Iterative Deepening Depth-First Search

It performs depth-first search to level 1, starts over, executes a complete depth-first search to level 2, and continues in such way till the solution is found.

It never creates a node until all lower nodes are generated. It only saves a stack of nodes. The algorithm ends when it finds a solution at depth d. The number of nodes created at depth d is b^d and at depth d-1 is b^{d-1}.

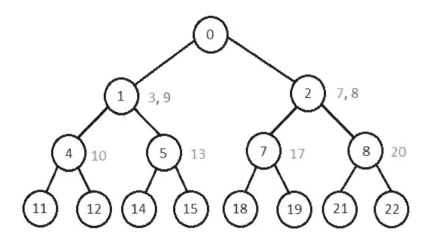

Comparison of Various Algorithms Complexities

Let us see the performance of algorithms based on various criteria:

Criterion	Breadth First	Depth First	Bidirectional	Uniform Cost	Iterative Deepening
Time	b^d	b^m	$b^{d/2}$	b^d	b^d
Space	b^d	b^m	$b^{d/2}$	b^d	b^d
Optimality	Y	N	Y	Y	Y
Completeness	Y	N	Y	Y	Y

Informed (Heuristic) Search Strategies

To solve large problems with large number of possible states, problem-specific knowledge needs to be added to increase the efficiency of search algorithms.

Heuristic Evaluation Functions

They calculate the cost of optimal path between two states. A heuristic function for sliding-tiles games is computed by counting number of moves that each tile makes from its goal state and adding these number of moves for all tiles.

Pure Heuristic Search

It expands nodes in the order of their heuristic values. It creates two lists, a closed list for the already expanded nodes and an open list for the created but unexpanded nodes.

In each iteration, a node with a minimum heuristic value is expanded, all its child nodes are created and placed in the closed list. Then, the heuristic function is applied to the child nodes and they are placed in the open list according to their heuristic value. The shorter paths are saved and the longer ones are disposed.

A* Search

It is best-known form of Best First search. It avoids expanding paths that are already expensive, but expands most promising paths first.

f(n) = g(n) + h(n), where

- g(n) the cost (so far) to reach the node

- h(n) estimated cost to get from the node to the goal

- f(n) estimated total cost of path through n to goal. It is implemented using priority queue by increasing f(n).

Greedy Best First Search

It expands the node that is estimated to be closest to goal. It expands nodes based on f(n) = h(n). It is implemented using priority queue.

Disadvantage: It can get stuck in loops. It is not optimal.

Local Search Algorithms

They start from a prospective solution and then move to a neighboring solution. They can return a valid solution even if it is interrupted at any time before they end.

Hill-Climbing Search

It is an iterative algorithm that starts with an arbitrary solution to a problem and attempts to find a better solution by changing a single element of the solution incrementally. If the change produces a better solution, an incremental change is taken as a new solution. This process is repeated until there are no further improvements.

function Hill-Climbing (problem), returns a state that is a local maximum.

inputs: problem, a problem

local variables: *current*, a node

           neighbor, a node

current ←Make_Node(Initial-State[problem])

loop

    do *neighbor* ← a highest_valued successor of *current*

        if Value[*neighbor*] ≤ Value[*current*] then

        return State[*current*]

        current ← *neighbor*

end

Disadvantage: This algorithm is neither complete, nor optimal.

Local Beam Search

In this algorithm, it holds k number of states at any given time. At the start, these states are generated randomly. The successors of these k states are computed with the help of objective function. If any of these successors is the maximum value of the objective function, then the algorithm stops.

Otherwise the (initial k states and k number of successors of the states = $2k$) states are placed in a pool. The pool is then sorted numerically. The highest k states are selected as new initial states. This process continues until a maximum value is reached.

function BeamSearch(*problem, k*), returns a solution state.

start with k randomly generated states

loop

    generate all successors of all k states

    if any of the states = solution, then return the state

    else select the k best successors

end

Simulated Annealing

Annealing is the process of heating and cooling a metal to change its internal structure for modifying its physical properties. When the metal cools, its new structure is seized, and the metal retains its newly obtained properties. In simulated annealing process, the temperature is kept variable.

We initially set the temperature high and then allow it to 'cool' slowly as the algorithm proceeds. When the temperature is high, the algorithm is allowed to accept worse solutions with high frequency.

Start

5. Initialize k = 0; L = integer number of variables;
6. From i -> j, search the performance difference Δ.
7. If $\Delta <= 0$ then accept else if $\exp(-\Delta/T(k)) > \text{random}(0,1)$ then accept;
8. Repeat steps 1 and 2 for L(k) steps.
9. k = k + 1;

Repeat steps 1 through 4 till the criteria is met.

End

Travelling Salesman Problem

In this algorithm, the objective is to find a low-cost tour that starts from a city, visits all cities en-route exactly once and ends at the same starting city.

Start

Find out all $(n-1)!$ Possible solutions, where n is the total number of cities.

Determine the minimum cost by finding out the cost of each of these (n -1)! solutions.

Finally, keep the one with the minimum cost.

end

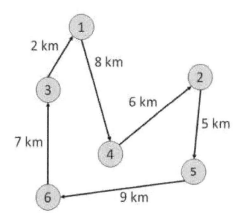

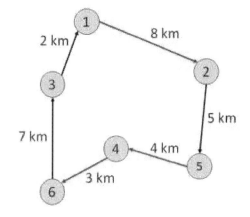

Total Distance = 37km   Total Distance = 31km

6.   Fuzzy Logic Systems

Fuzzy Logic Systems (FLS) produce acceptable but definite output in response to incomplete, ambiguous, distorted, or inaccurate (fuzzy) input.

What is Fuzzy Logic?

Fuzzy Logic (FL) is a method of reasoning that resembles human reasoning. The approach of FL imitates the way of decision making in humans that involves all intermediate possibilities between digital values YES and NO.

The conventional logic block that a computer can understand takes precise input and produces a definite output as TRUE or FALSE, which is equivalent to human's YES or NO.

The inventor of fuzzy logic, Lotfi Zadeh, observed that unlike computers, the human decision making includes a range of possibilities between YES and NO, such as:

CERTAINLY YES
POSSIBLY YES
CANNOT SAY
POSSIBLY NO
CERTAINLY NO

The fuzzy logic works on the levels of possibilities of input to achieve the definite output.

Implementation
- It can be implemented in systems with various sizes and capabilities ranging from small micro-controllers to large, networked, workstation-based control systems.
- It can be implemented in hardware, software, or a combination of both.

Why Fuzzy Logic?

Fuzzy logic is useful for commercial and practical purposes.

- It can control machines and consumer products.
- It may not give accurate reasoning, but acceptable reasoning.
- Fuzzy logic helps to deal with the uncertainty in engineering.

Fuzzy Logic Systems Architecture

It has four main parts as shown:

1. **Fuzzification Module:** transforms the system inputs, which are crisp numbers, into fuzzy sets.

   It splits the input signal into five steps such as:

LP	x is Large Positive
MP	x is Medium Positive
S	x is Small
MN	x is Medium Negative
LN	x is Large Negative

2. **Knowledge Base:** It stores IF-THEN rules provided by experts.
3. **Inference Engine:** It simulates the human reasoning process by making fuzzy inference on the inputs and IF-THEN rules.
4. **Defuzzification Module:** It transforms the fuzzy set obtained by the inference engine into a crisp value.

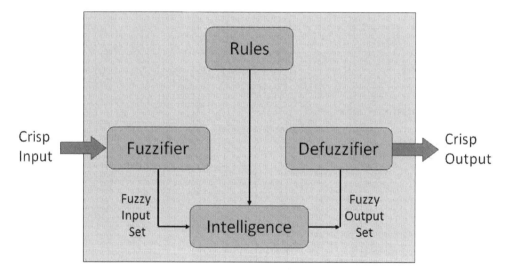

These **membership functions work on** fuzzy sets of variables.

Membership Functions

Membership functions allow you to graphically. A **membership function** defined as $\mu_A:X \rightarrow [0,1]$. quantify linguistic term and represent a fuzzy set for a fuzzy set A on the universe of discourse X is

Here, each element of X is mapped to a value between 0 and 1. It is called **membership value** or degree of membership. It quantifies the degree of membership of the element in X to the fuzzy set A.

- x axis represents the universe of discourse.
- y axis represents the degrees of membership in the [0, 1] interval.

There can be multiple membership functions applicable to fuzzify a numerical value. Simple membership functions are used as use of complex functions does not add more precision in the output.

All membership functions for **LP, MP, S, MN,** and **LN** are shown as below:

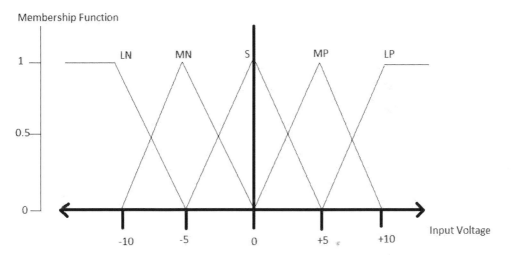

The triangular membership function shapes are most common among various other membership function shapes such as trapezoidal, singleton, and Gaussian.

Here, the input to 5-level fuzzifier varies from -10 volts to +10 volts. Hence the corresponding output also changes.

Example of a Fuzzy Logic System

Let us consider an air conditioning system with 5-lvel fuzzy logic system. This system adjusts the temperature of air conditioner by comparing the room temperature and the target temperature value.

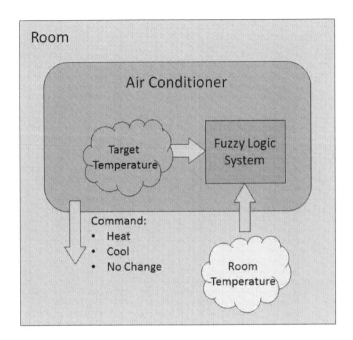

Algorithm

1. Define linguistic Variables and terms (start)
2. Construct membership functions for them. (start)
3. Construct knowledge base of rules (start)
4. Convert crisp data into fuzzy data sets using membership functions (fuzzification)
5. Evaluate rules in the rule base (inference engine)
6. Combine results from each rule (inference engine)
7. Convert output data into non-fuzzy values. (defuzzification)

Development

Step 1: Define linguistic variables and terms

Linguistic variables are input and output variables in the form of simple words or sentences. For room temperature, cold, warm, hot, etc., are linguistic terms.

Temperature (t) = {very-cold, cold, warm, very-warm, hot}

Every member of this set is a linguistic term and it can cover some portion of overall temperature values.

Step 2: Construct membership functions for them

The membership functions of temperature variable are as shown:

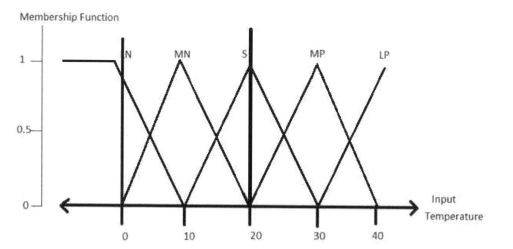

Step3: Construct knowledge base rules

Create a matrix of room temperature values versus target temperature values that an air conditioning system is expected to provide.

RoomTemp/Target	Very_Cold	Cold	Warm	Hot	Very_Hot
Very_Cold	No_Change	Heat	Heat	Heat	Heat
Cold	Cool	No_Change	Heat	Heat	Heat
Warm	Cool	Cool	No_Change	Heat	Heat
Hot	Cool	Cool	Cool	No_Change	Heat
Very_Hot	Cool	Cool	Cool	Cool	No_Change

Build a set of rules into the knowledge base in the form of IF-THEN-ELSE structures.

Sr. No.	Condition	Action
1	IF temperature=(Cold OR Very_Cold) AND target=Warm THEN	HEAT
2	IF temperature=(Hot OR Very_Hot) AND target=Warm THEN	COOL
3	IF (temperature=Warm) AND (target=Warm) THEN	NOCHANGE

Step5

Fuzzy set operations perform evaluation of rules. The operations used for OR and AND are Max and Min respectively. All results of evaluation are combined to form a final result. This result is a fuzzy value.

Step 6

Defuzzification is then performed according to membership function for output variable.

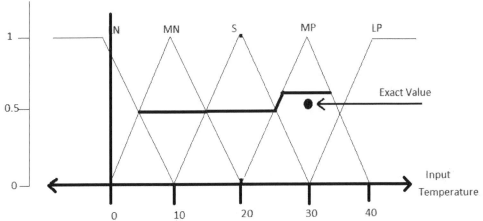

Application Areas of Fuzzy Logic

The key application areas of fuzzy logic are as given:

Automotive Systems

- Automatic Gearboxes
- Four-Wheel Steering
- Vehicle environment control

Consumer Electronics

- Hi-Fi Systems
- Photocopiers
- Still and Video Cameras
- Television

Domestic Goods

- Microwave Ovens
- Refrigerators
- Toasters
- Vacuum Cleaners

- Washing Machines

Environment Control

- Air Conditioners/Dryers/Heaters
- Humidifiers

Advantages of FLSs

- Mathematical concepts within fuzzy reasoning are very simple.
- You can modify a FIS by just adding or deleting rules due to flexibility of fuzzy logic.
- Fuzzy logic Systems can take imprecise, distorted, noisy input information.
- FLSs are easy to construct and understand.
- Fuzzy logic is a solution to complex problems in all fields of life, including medicine, as it resembles human reasoning and decision making.

Disadvantages of FLSs

- There is no systematic approach to fuzzy system designing.
- They are understandable only when simple.
- They are suitable for the problems which do not need high accuracy.

7. Natural Language Processing

Natural Language Processing (NLP) refers to AI method of communicating with an intelligent systems using a natural language such as English.

Processing of Natural Language is required when you want an intelligent system like robot to perform as per your instructions, when you want to hear decision from a dialogue based clinical expert system, etc.

The field of NLP involves making computers to perform useful tasks with the natural languages humans use. The input and output of an NLP system can be:

- Speech
- Written Text

Components of NLP

There are two components of NLP as given:

Natural Language Understanding (NLU)

Understanding involves the following tasks:

- Mapping the given input in natural language into useful representations.
- Analyzing different aspects of the language.

Natural Language Generation (NLG)

It is the process of producing meaningful phrases and sentences in the form of natural language from some internal representation.

It involves:

- **Text planning:** It includes retrieving the relevant content from knowledge base.
- **Sentence planning:** It includes choosing required words, forming meaningful phrases, setting tone of the sentence.
- **Text Realization:** It is mapping sentence plan into sentence structure.

The NLU is harder than NLG.

Difficulties in NLU

- NL has an extremely rich form and structure.
- It is very ambiguous. There can be different levels of ambiguity:
  - **Lexical ambiguity:** It is at very primitive level such as word-level.

34

- o   For example, treating the word "board" as noun or verb?
- o   **Syntax Level ambiguity**: A sentence can be parsed in different ways.
- o   For example, "He lifted the beetle with red cap." – Did he use cap to lift the beetle or he lifted a beetle that had red cap?
- o   **Referential ambiguity**: Referring to something using pronouns. For example, Rima went to Gauri. She said, "I am tired." - Exactly who is tired?
- o   One input can mean different meanings. o
  Many inputs can mean the same thing.

NLP Terminology

- **Phonology:** It is study of organizing sound systematically.
- **Morphology:** It is a study of construction of words from primitive meaningful units.
- **Morpheme:** It is primitive unit of meaning in a language.
- **Syntax:** It refers to arranging words to make a sentence. It also involves determining the structural role of words in the sentence and in phrases.
- **Semantics:** It is concerned with the meaning of words and how to combine words into meaningful phrases and sentences.
- **Pragmatics:** It deals with using and understanding sentences in different situations and how the interpretation of the sentence is affected.
- **Discourse**: It deals with how the immediately preceding sentence can affect the interpretation of the next sentence.
- **World Knowledge:** It includes the general knowledge about the world.

Steps in NLP

There are general five steps:

1. **Lexical Analysis**
   It involves identifying and analyzing the structure of words. Lexicon of a language means the collection of words and phrases in a language. Lexical analysis is dividing the whole chunk of txt into paragraphs, sentences, and words.
2. **Syntactic Analysis (Parsing)**
   It involves analysis of words in the sentence for grammar and arranging words in a manner that shows the relationship among the words. The sentence such as "The school goes to boy" is rejected by English syntactic analyzer.

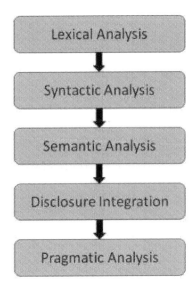

3. **Semantic Analysis**
   It draws the exact meaning or the dictionary meaning from the text. The text is checked for meaningfulness. It is done by mapping syntactic structures and objects in the task domain. The semantic analyzer disregards sentence such as "hot ice-cream".

4. **Discourse Integration**
   The meaning of any sentence depends upon the meaning of the sentence just before it. In addition, it also brings about the meaning of immediately succeeding sentence.

5. **Pragmatic Analysis**
   During this, what was said is re-interpreted on what it actually meant. It involves deriving those aspects of language which require real world knowledge.

Implementation Aspects of Syntactic Analysis

There are a number of algorithms researchers have developed for syntactic analysis, but we consider only the following simple methods:

- Context-Free Grammar
- Top-Down Parser

Let us see them in detail:

Context-Free Grammar

It is the grammar that consists rules with a single symbol on the left-hand side of the rewrite rules. Let us create grammar to parse a sentence –

"The bird pecks the grains"

Articles (DET): a | an | the.

Nouns: bird | birds | grain | grains

Noun Phrase (NP): Article + Noun | Article + Adjective + Noun

= DET N | DET ADJ N

Verbs: pecks | pecking | pecked

Verb Phrase (VP): NP V | V NP

Adjectives (ADJ): beautiful | small | chirping

The parse tree breaks down the sentence into structured parts so that the computer can easily understand and process it. In order for the parsing algorithm to construct this parse tree, a set of rewrite rules, which describe what tree structures are legal, need to be constructed.

These rules say that a certain symbol may be expanded in the tree by a sequence of other symbols. According to first order logic rule, ff there are two strings Noun Phrase (NP) and Verb Phrase (VP), then the string combined by NP followed by VP is a sentence. The rewrite rules for the sentence are as follows:

S -> NP VP
NP -> DET N | DET ADJ N
VP -> V NP

Lexocon:
DET -> a | the
ADJ -> beautiful | perching
N -> bird | birds | grain | grains

V -> peck | pecks | pecking

The parse tree can be created as shown:

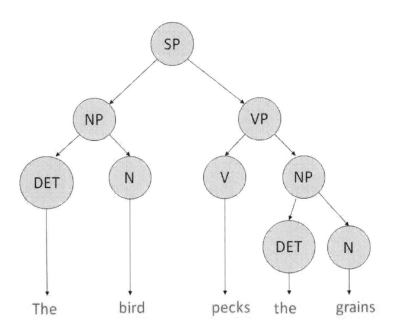

Now consider the above rewrite rules. Since *V* can be replaced by both, "peck" or "pecks", sentences such as "The *bird peck* the grains" can be wrongly permitted. i. e. the subject-verb agreement error is approved as correct.

Merit: The simplest style of grammar, therefore widely used one.

Demerits:

- They are not highly precise. For example, "The *grains peck the bird*", is a syntactically correct according to parser, but even if it makes no sense, parser takes it as a correct sentence.

- To bring out high precision, multiple sets of grammar need to be prepared. It may require a completely different sets of rules for parsing singular and plural variations, passive sentences, etc., which can lead to creation of huge set of rules that are unmanageable.

Top-Down Parser

Here, the parser starts with the *S* symbol and attempts to rewrite it into a sequence

of *terminal symbols* that matches the classes of the words in the input sentence until it consists entirely of terminal symbols.

These are then checked with the input sentence to see if it matched. If not, the process is started over again with a different set of rules. This is repeated until a specific rule is found which describes the structure of the sentence.

Merit: It is simple to implement.

Demerits:

- It is inefficient, as the search process has to be repeated if an error occurs.
- Slow speed of working.

8. Expert Systems

Expert systems (ES) are one of the prominent research domains of AI. It is introduced by the researchers at Stanford University, Computer Science Department.

What are Expert Systems?

The expert systems are the computer applications developed to solve complex problems in a particular domain, at the level of extra-ordinary human intelligence and expertise.

Characteristics of Expert Systems
- High performance
- Understandable
- Reliable
- Highly responsive

Capabilities of Expert Systems

The expert systems are capable of:

- Advising
- Instructing and assisting human in decision making
- Demonstrating
- Deriving a solution
- Diagnosing
- Explaining
- Interpreting input
- Predicting results
- Justifying the conclusion
- Suggesting alternative options to a problem

They are incapable of:

- Substituting human decision makers
- Possessing human capabilities
- Producing accurate output for inadequate knowledge base
- Refining their own knowledge

Components of Expert Systems

The components of ES include:

- Knowledge Base
- Inference Engine
- User Interface

Let us see them one by one briefly:

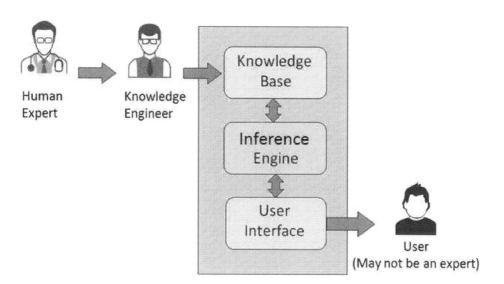

Knowledge Base

It contains domain-specific and high-quality knowledge.

Knowledge is required to exhibit intelligence. The success of any ES majorly depends upon the collection of highly accurate and precise knowledge.

What is Knowledge?

The data is collection of facts. The information is organized as data and facts about the task domain. **Data**, **information**, and **past experience** combined together are termed as knowledge.

Components of Knowledge Base

The knowledge base of an ES is a store of both, factual and heuristic knowledge.

- **Factual Knowledge** – It is the information widely accepted by the Knowledge Engineers and scholars in the task domain.

- **Heuristic Knowledge** – It is about practice, accurate judgment, one's ability of evaluation, and guessing.

Knowledge representation

It is the method used to organize and formalize the knowledge in the knowledge base. It is in the form of IF-THEN-ELSE rules.

Knowledge Acquisition

The success of any expert system majorly depends on the quality, completeness, and accuracy of the information stored in the knowledge base.

The knowledge base is formed by readings from various experts, scholars, and the **Knowledge Engineers**. The knowledge engineer is a person with the qualities of empathy, quick learning, and case analyzing skills.

He acquires information from subject expert by recording, interviewing, and observing him at work, etc. He then categorizes and organizes the information in a meaningful way, in the form of IF-THEN-ELSE rules, to be used by interference machine. The knowledge engineer also monitors the development of the ES.

Inference Engine

Use of efficient procedures and rules by the Inference Engine is essential in deducting a correct, flawless solution.

In case of knowledge-based ES, the Inference Engine acquires and manipulates the knowledge from the knowledge base to arrive at a particular solution.

In case of rule based ES, it:

- Applies rules repeatedly to the facts, which are obtained from earlier rule application.
- Adds new knowledge into the knowledge base if required.
- Resolves rules conflict when multiple rules are applicable to a particular case

To recommend a solution, the inference engine uses the following strategies:

- Forward Chaining
- Backward Chaining

Forward Chaining

It is a strategy of an expert system to answer the question, **"What can happen next?"**

Here, the inferance engine follows the chain of conditions and derivations and finally deduces the outcome. It considers all the facts and rules, and sorts them before concluding to a solution.

This strategy is followed for working on conclusion, result, or effect. For example, prediction of share market status as an effect of changes in interest rates.

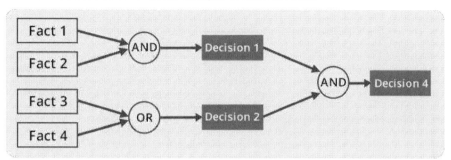

Backward Chaining

With this strategy, an expert system finds out the answer to the question, **"Why this happened?"**

On the basis of what has already happened, the inference engine tries to find out which conditions could have happened in the past for this result. This strategy is followed for finding out cause or reason. For example, diagnosis of blood cancer in humans.

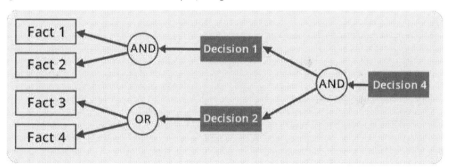

User Interface

User interface provides interaction between user of the ES and the ES itself. It is generally Natural Language Processing so as to be used by the user who is well-versed in the task domain. The user of the ES need not be necessarily an expert in Artificial Intelligence.

It explains how the ES has arrived at a particular recommendation. The explanation may in the following forms:

- Natural language displayed on screen
- Verbal narrations in natural language

- Listing of rule numbers displayed on the screen.

The user interface makes it easy to trace the credibility of the deductions.

Requirements of Efficient ES User Interface
- It should help users to accomplish their goals in shortest possible ay.
- It should be designed to work for user's existing or desired work practices.
- Its technology should be adaptable to user's requirements; not the other way round.
- It should make efficient use of user input.

Expert Systems Limitations

No technology can offer easy and complete solution. Large systems are costly, require significant development time, and computer resources. ESs have their limitations which include:

- Limitations of the technology
- Difficult knowledge acquisition
- ES are Difficult to maintain
- High Development costs

Applications of Expert System

The following table shows where ES can be applied.

Application	Description
Design Domain	Camera lens design, automobile design.
Medical Domain	Diagnosis Systems to deduce cause of disease from observed data, conduction medical operations on humans.
Monitoring Systems	Comparing data continuously with observed system or with prescribed behavior such as leakage monitoring in long petroleum pipeline.
Process Control Systems	Controlling a physical process based on monitoring.
Knowledge Domain	Finding out faults in vehicles, computers.
Finance/Commerce	Detection of possible fraud, suspicious transactions, stock market trading, Airline scheduling, cargo scheduling.

Expert System Technology

There are several levels of ES technologies available. Expert systems technologies include:

1. **Expert System Development Environment:** The ES development environment includes hardware and tools. They are:

   o Workstations, minicomputers, mainframes

   o High level Symbolic Programming Languages such as **LIS**t **P**rogramming (LISP) and **PRO**grammation en **LOG**ique (PROLOG).

   o Large databases

2. **Tools:** They reduce the effort and cost involved in developing an expert system to large extent.

   o Powerful editors and debugging tools with multi-windows.

   o They provide rapid prototyping

   o Have Inbuilt definitions of model, knowledge representation, and inference design.

1. **Shells:** A shell is nothing but an expert system without knowledge base. A shell provides the developers with knowledge acquisition, inference engine, user interface, and explanation facility. For example, few shells are given below:

   o Java Expert System Shell (JESS) that provides fully developed Java API for creating an expert system.

   o *Vidwan*, a shell developed at the National Centre for Software Technology, Mumbai in 1993. It enables knowledge encoding in the form of IF-THEN rules.

Development of Expert Systems: General Steps

The process of ES development is iterative. Steps in developing the ES include:

1. Identify Problem Domain

- The problem must be suitable for an expert system to solve it.
- Find the experts in task domain for the ES project.
- Establish cost-effectiveness of the system.

2. Design the System

- Identify the ES Technology.
- Know and establish the degree of integration with the other systems and databases.
- Realize how the concepts can represent the domain knowledge best.

3. Develop the Prototype

Form Knowledge Base: The knowledge engineer works to:

- Acquire domain knowledge from the expert.
- Represent it in the form of If-THEN-ELSE rules.

4. Test and Refine the Prototype

- The knowledge engineer uses sample cases to test the prototype for any deficiencies in performance.
- End users test the prototypes of the ES.

5. Develop and Complete the ES

- Test and ensure the interaction of the ES with all elements of its environment, including end users, databases, and other information systems.
- Document the ES project well.
- Train the user to use ES.

6. Maintain the System

- Keep the knowledge base up-to-date by regular review and update.
- Cater for new interfaces with other information systems, as those systems evolve.

Benefits of Expert Systems

- **Availability:** They are easily available due to mass production of software.
- **Less Production Cost:** Production cost is reasonable. This makes them affordable.
- **Speed:** They offer great speed. They reduce the amount of work an individual puts in.
- **Less Error Rate:** Error rate is low as compared to human errors.
- **Reducing Risk:** They can work in the environment dangerous to humans.
- **Steady response:** They work steadily without getting motional, tensed or fatigued.

9. Robotics

Robotics is a domain in artificial intelligence that deals with the study of creating intelligent and efficient robots.

What are Robots?

Robots are the artificial agents acting in real world environment.

Objective

Robots are aimed at manipulating the objects by perceiving, picking, moving, modifying the physical properties of object, destroying it, or to have an effect thereby freeing manpower from doing repetitive functions without getting bored, distracted, or exhausted.

What is Robotics?

Robotics is a branch of AI, which is composed of Electrical Engineering, Mechanical Engineering, and Computer Science for designing, construction, and application of robots.

Aspects of Robotics

* The robots have **mechanical construction**, form, or shape designed to accomplish a particular task.
* They have **electrical components** which power and control the machinery.
* They contain some level of **computer program** that determines what, when and how a robot does something.

Difference in Robot System and Other AI Program

Here is the difference between the two:

AI Programs	Robots
They usually operate in computer-stimulated worlds.	They operate in real physical world
The input to an AI program is in symbols and rules.	Inputs to robots is analog signal in the form of speech waveform or images
They need general purpose computers to operate on.	They need special hardware with sensors and effectors.

Robot Locomotion

Locomotion is the mechanism that makes a robot capable of moving in its environment. There are various types of locomotions:

- Legged
- Wheeled
- Combination of Legged and Wheeled Locomotion
- Tracked slip/skid

Legged Locomotion

- This type of locomotion consumes more power while demonstrating walk, jump, trot, hop, climb up or down, etc.
- It requires more number of motors to accomplish a movement. It is suited for rough as well as smooth terrain where irregular or too smooth surface makes it consume more power for a wheeled locomotion. It is little difficult to implement because of stability issues.
- It comes with the variety of one, two, four, and six legs. If a robot has multiple legs then leg coordination is necessary for locomotion.

The total number of possible **gaits** (a periodic sequence of lift and release events for each of the total legs) a robot can travel depends upon the number of its legs.

If a robot has k legs, then the number of possible events $N = (2k-1)!$.

In case of a two-legged robot ($k=2$), the number of possible events is $N = (2k-1)!$

$= (2*2-1)! = 3! = 6$.

Hence there are six possible different events:

1. Lifting the Left leg

2. Releasing the Left leg

3. Lifting the Right leg

4. Releasing the Right leg

5. Lifting both the legs together

6. Releasing both the legs together.

In case of k=6 legs, there are 39916800 possible events. Hence the complexity of robots is directly proportional to the number of legs.

Wheeled Locomotion

It requires fewer number of motors to accomplish a movement. It is little easy to implement as there are less stability issues in case of more number of wheels. It is power efficient as compared to legged locomotion.

- **Standard wheel:** Rotates around the wheel axle and around the contact
- **Castor wheel:** Rotates around the wheel axle and the offset steering joint
- **Swedish 45° and Swedish 90° wheels:** Omni-wheel, rotates around the contact point, around the wheel axle, and around the rollers.
- **Ball or spherical wheel:** Omnidirectional wheel, technically difficult to implement.

Slip/Skid Locomotion

In this type, the vehicles use tracks as in a tank. The robot is steered by moving the tracks with different speeds in the same or opposite direction. It offers stability because of large contact area of track and ground.

Components of a Robot

Robots are constructed with the following:

- **Power Supply:** The robots are powered by batteries, solar power, hydraulic, or pneumatic power sources.
- **Actuators**: They convert energy into movement.
- **Electric motors (AC/DC):** They are required for rotational movement.
- **Pneumatic Air Muscles**: They contract almost 40% when air is sucked in them.
- **Muscle Wires**: They contract by 5% when electric current is passed through them.
- **Piezo Motors and Ultrasonic Motors**: Best for industrial robots.
- **Sensors**: They provide knowledge of real time information on the task environment. Robots are equipped with vision sensors to be to compute the depth in the environment. A tactile sensor imitates the mechanical properties of touch receptors of human fingertips.

Computer Vision

This is a technology of AI with which the robots can see. The computer vision plays vital role in the domains of safety, security, health, access, and entertainment.

Computer vision automatically extracts, analyzes, and comprehends useful information from a single image or an array of images. This process involves development of algorithms to accomplish automatic visual comprehension.

Hardware of Computer Vision System

This involves:

- Power supply
- Image acquisition device such as camera
- a processor
- a software
- A display device for monitoring the system
- Accessories such as camera stands, cables, and connectors

Tasks of Computer Vision

OCR: In the domain of computers, Optical Character Reader, a software to convert scanned documents into editable text, which accompanies a scanner.

Face Detection: Many state-of-the-art cameras come with this feature, which enables to read the face and take the picture of that perfect expression. It is used to let a user access the software on correct match.

Object Recognition: They are installed in supermarkets, cameras, high-end cars such as BMW, GM, and Volvo.

Estimating Position: It is estimating position of an object with respect to camera as in position of tumor in human's body.

Application Domains of Computer Vision

- agriculture
- autonomous vehicles
- biometrics
- character recognition
- forensics, security, and surveillance
- industrial quality inspection
- face recognition
- gesture analysis
- geoscience
- medical imagery
- pollution monitoring
- process control
- remote sensing
- robotics
- transport

Applications of Robotics

The robotics has been instrumental in the various domains such as:

- **Industries:** Robots are used for handling material, cutting, welding, color coating, drilling, polishing, etc.
- **Military:** Autonomous robots can reach inaccessible and hazardous zones during war. A robot named *Daksh*, developed by Defense Research and Development Organization (DRDO), is in function to destroy life-threatening objects safely.
- **Medicine:** The robots are capable of carrying out hundreds of clinical tests simultaneously, rehabilitating permanently disabled people, and performing complex surgeries such as brain tumors.

- **Exploration:** The robot rock climbers used for space exploration, underwater drones used for ocean exploration are to name a few.
- **Entertainment:** Disney's engineers have created hundreds of robots for movie making.

10. Neural Networks

Yet another research area in AI, neural networks, is inspired from the natural neural network of human nervous system.

What are Artificial Neural Networks (ANNs)?

The inventor of the first neurocomputer, Dr. Robert Hecht-Nielsen, defines a neural network as:

"...a computing system made up of a number of simple, highly interconnected processing elements, which process information by their dynamic state response to external inputs."

Basic Structure of ANNs

The idea of ANNs is based on the belief that working of human brain by making the right connections, can be imitated using silicon and wires as living **neurons and dendrites**.

The human brain is composed of 100 billion nerve cells called **neurons**. They are connected to other thousand cells by **Axons**. Stimuli from external environment or inputs from sensory organs are accepted by dendrites. These inputs create electric impulses, which quickly travel through the neural network. A neuron can then send the message to other neuron to handle the issue or does not send it forward.

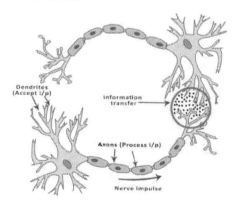

ANNs are composed of multiple **nodes,** which imitate biological **neurons** of human brain. The neurons are connected by links and they interact with each other. The nodes can take input data and perform simple operations on the data. The result of these operations is passed to other neurons. The output at each node is called its **activation** or **node value**.

Each link is associated with **weight**. ANNs are capable of learning, which takes place by altering weight values. The following illustration shows a simple ANN:

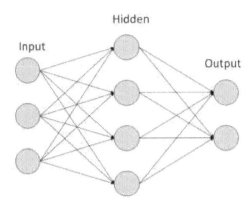

Types of Artificial Neural Networks

There are two Artificial Neural Network topologies: **FeedForward** and **Feedback**.

FeedForward ANN

In this ANN, the information flow is unidirectional. A unit sends information to other unit from which it does not receive any information. There are no feedback loops. They are used in pattern generation/recognition/classification. They have fixed inputs and outputs.

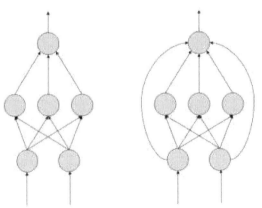

Feedback ANN

Here, feedback loops are allowed. They are used in content addressable memories.

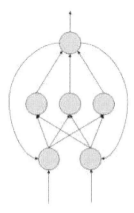

Working of ANNs

In the topology diagrams shown, each arrow represents a connection between two neurons and indicates the pathway for the flow of information. Each connection has a weight, an integer number that controls the signal between the two neurons.

If the network generates a "good or desired" output, there is no need to adjust the weights. However, if the network generates a "poor or undesired" output or an error, then the system alters the weights in order to improve subsequent results.

Machine Learning in ANNs

ANNs are capable of learning and they need to be trained. There are several learning strategies:

- **Supervised Learning:** It involves a teacher that is scholar than the ANN itself. For example, the teacher feeds some example data about which the teacher already knows the answers.

  For example, pattern recognizing. The ANN comes up with guesses while recognizing. Then the teacher provides the ANN with the answers. The network then compares it guesses with the teacher's "correct" answers and makes adjustments according to errors.

- **Unsupervised Learning:** It is required when there is no example data set with known answers. For example, searching for a hidden pattern. In this case, clustering i.e. dividing a set of elements into groups according to some unknown pattern is carried out based on the existing data sets present.

- **Reinforcement Learning:** This strategy built on observation. The ANN makes a decision by observing its environment. If the observation is negative, the network adjusts its weights to be able to make a different required decision the next time.

Back Propagation Algorithm

It is the training or learning algorithm. It learns by example. If you submit to the algorithm the example of what you want the network to do, it changes the network's weights so that it can produce desired output for a particular input on finishing the training.

Back Propagation networks are ideal for simple Pattern Recognition and Mapping Tasks.

Bayesian Networks (BN)

These are the graphical structures used to represent the probabilistic relationship among a set of random variables. Bayesian networks are also called **Belief Networks** or **Bayes Nets**. BNs reason about uncertain domain.

In these networks, each node represents a random variable with specific propositions. For example, in a medical diagnosis domain, the node *Cancer* represents the proposition that a patient has cancer.

The edges connecting the nodes represent probabilistic dependencies among those random variables. If out of two nodes, one is affecting the other then they must be directly connected in the directions of the effect. The strength of the relationship between variables is quantified by the probability associated with each node.

There is an only constraint on the arcs in a BN that you cannot return to a node simply by following directed arcs. Hence the BNs are called Directed Acyclic Graphs (DAGs).

BNs are capable of handling multivalued variables simultaneously. The BN variables are composed of two dimensions:

1. Range of prepositions
2. Probability assigned to each of the prepositions.

Consider a finite set $X = \{X_1, X_2, ...,X_n\}$ of discrete random variables, where each variable X_i may take values from a finite set, denoted by *Val(Xi)*. If there is a directed link from variable X_i to variable, X_j, then variable X_i will be a parent of variable X_j showing direct dependencies between the variables.

The structure of BN is ideal for combining prior knowledge and observed data. BN can be used to learn the causal relationships and understand various problem domains and to predict future events, even in case of missing data.

Building a Bayesian Network

A knowledge engineer can build a Bayesian network. There are a number of steps the knowledge engineer needs to take while building it.

Example problem: *Lung cancer.* A patient has been suffering from breathlessness. He visits the doctor, suspecting he has lung cancer. The doctor knows that barring lung cancer, there are various other possible diseases the patient might have such as tuberculosis and bronchitis.

Gather Relevant Information of Problem

- Is the patient a smoker? If yes, then high chances of cancer and bronchitis.
- Is the patient exposed to air pollution? If yes, what sort of air pollution?
- Take an X-Ray positive X-ray would indicate either TB or lung cancer.

Identify Interesting Variables

The knowledge engineer tries to answer the questions:

- Which nodes to represent?
- What values can they take? In which state can they be?

For now let us consider nodes, with only discrete values. The variable must take on exactly one of these values at a time.

Common types of discrete nodes are:

- **Boolean nodes:** They represent propositions, taking binary values TRUE (T) and FALSE (F).

- **Ordered values:** A node *Pollution* might represent and take values from {low, medium, high} describing degree of a patient's exposure to pollution.

- **Integral values:** A node called *Age* might represent patient's age with possible values from 1 to 120. Even at this early stage, modeling choices are being made.

Possible nodes and values for the lung cancer example:

Node Name	Type	Value	
Pollution	Binary	{LOW, HIGH, MEDIUM}	
Smoker	Boolean	{TRUE, FASLE}	
Lung-Cancer	Boolean	{TRUE, FASLE}	
X-Ray	Binary	{Positive, Negative}	

Create Arcs between Nodes

Topology of the network should capture qualitative relationships between variables.

For example, what causes a patient to have lung cancer? - Pollution and smoking. Then add arcs from node *Pollution* and node *Smoker* to node *Lung-Cancer*.

Similarly if patient has lung cancer, then X-ray result will be positive. Then add arcs from *Lung-Cancer* to *X-Ray*.

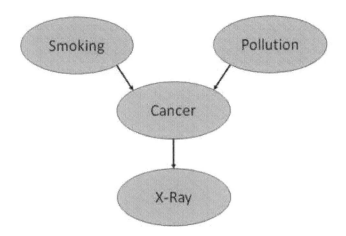

Specify Topology

Conventionally, BNs are laid out so that the arcs point from top to bottom. The set of parent nodes of a node X is given by Parents(X).

The *Lung-Cancer* node has two parents (reasons or causes): *Pollution* and *Smoker*, while node *Smoker* is an **ancestor** of node *X-Ray*. Similarly, *X-Ray* is a child (consequence or effects) of node *Lung-Cancer* and **successor** of nodes *Smoker* and *Pollution*.

Conditional Probabilities

Now quantify the relationships between connected nodes: this is done by specifying a conditional probability distribution for each node. As only discrete variables are considered here, this takes the form of a **Conditional Probability Table (CPT)**.

First, for each node we need to look at all the possible combinations of values of those parent nodes. Each such combination is called an **instantiation** of the parent set. For each distinct instantiation of parent node values, we need to specify the probability that the child will take.

For example, the *Lung-Cancer* node's parents are *Pollution* and *Smoking*. They take the possible values = { (H,T), (H,F), (L,T), (L,F)}. The CPT specifies the probability of cancer for each of these cases as <0.05, 0.02, 0.03, 0.001> respectively.

Each node will have conditional probability associated as follows:

Smoking	Pollution
P(S = T)	P(P = L)
0.30	0.90

Lung-Cancer		
P	S	P (C = T|P, S)
H	T	0.05
H	F	0.02
L	T	0.03
L	F	0.001

X-Ray	
C	X = (Pos | C)
T	0.90
F	0.20

Applications of Neural Networks

They can perform tasks that are easy for a human but difficult for a machine:

- **Aerospace**: Autopilot aircrafts, aircraft fault detection.
- **Automotive:** Automobile guidance systems.
- **Military**: Weapon steering, target tracking, object discrimination, facial recognition, signal/image identification.
- **Electronics:** Code sequence prediction, IC chip layout, chip failure analysis, machine vision, voice synthesis.
- **Financial:** Real estate appraisal, loan advisor, mortgage screening, corporate bond rating, portfolio trading program, corporate financial analysis, currency value prediction, document readers, credit application evaluators.
- **Industrial:** Manufacturing process control, product design and analysis, quality inspection systems, welding quality analysis, paper quality prediction, chemical product design analysis, dynamic modeling of chemical process systems, machine maintenance analysis, project bidding, planning, and management.

- **Medical:** Cancer cell analysis, EEG and ECG analysis, prosthetic design, transplant time optimizer.
- **Speech:** Speech recognition, speech classification, text to speech conversion.
- **Telecommunications**: Image and data compression, automated information services, real-time spoken language translation.
- **Transportation:** Truck brake diagnosis, vehicle scheduling, routing systems.
- **Software:** Pattern Recognition in facial recognition, optical character recognition, etc.
- **Time Series Prediction:** ANNs are used to make predictions on stocks and natural calamities.
- **Signal Processing**: Neural networks can be trained to process an audio signal and filter it appropriately in the hearing aids.
- **Control:** ANNs are often used to make steering decisions of physical vehicles.
- **Anomaly Detection:** As ANNs are expert at recognizing patterns, they can also be trained to generate an output when something unusual occurs that misfits the pattern.

11. AI Issues

AI is developing with such an incredible speed, sometimes it seems magical. There is an opinion among researchers and developers that AI could grow so immensely strong that it would be difficult for humans to control.

Humans developed AI systems by introducing into them every possible intelligence they could, for which the humans themselves now seem threatened.

Threat to Privacy

An AI program that recognizes speech and understands natural language is theoretically capable of understanding each conversation on e-mails and telephones.

Threat to Human Dignity

AI systems have already started replacing the human beings in few industries. It should not replace people in the sectors where they are holding dignified positions which are pertaining to ethics such as nursing, surgeon, judge, police officer, etc.

Threat to Safety

The self-improving AI systems can become so mighty than humans that could be very difficult to stop from achieving their goals, which may lead to unintended consequences.

12. AI Terminology

Here is the list of frequently used terms in the domain of AI:

Term	Meaning
Agent	Agents are systems or software programs capable of autonomous, purposeful and reasoning directed towards one or more goals. They are also called assistants, brokers, bots, droids, intelligent agents, and software agents.
Autonomous Robot	Robot free from external control or influence and able to control itself independently.
Backward Chaining	Strategy of working backward for Reason/Cause of a problem.
Blackboard	It is the memory inside computer, which is used for communication between the cooperating expert systems.
Environment	It is the part of real or computational world inhabited by the agent.
Forward Chaining	Strategy of working forward for conclusion/solution of a problem.
Heuristics	It is the knowledge based on Trial-and-error, evaluations, and experimentation.
Knowledge Engineering	Acquiring knowledge from human experts and other resources.
Percepts	It is the format in which the agent obtains information about the environment.
Pruning	Overriding unnecessary and irrelevant considerations in AI systems.
Rule	It is a format of representing knowledge base in Expert System. It is in the form of IF-THEN-ELSE.
Shell	A shell is a software that helps in designing inference engine, knowledge base, and user interface of an expert system.
Task	It is the goal the agent is tries to accomplish.
Turing Test	A test developed by Allan Turing to test the intelligence of a machine as compared to human intelligence.

Printed in Great Britain
by Amazon